Baked apples and bus tours

Jan Oskar Hansen

The Author

Jan Oskar Hansen is a poet, story teller and seafarer, born in Stavanger, Norway. He joined the merchant navy at 15 and spent most of his life at sea until settling in the early 90's in Portugal. His poetry has been widely published in hard copy and online, worldwide. Reviewers have generally commented that a love and honoring of living things stands out in Hansen's work, and deep humility; that it reveals with unflinching honesty man's shortcomings in his efforts to love, telling what there is to tell in a first person, deeply resident universal voice.

The poet is widely read and fluent in several languages, knowledge often acquired at night during his many years at sea. He chose to write primarily in English following enthusiastic reception of his work from English-speaking editors and readers.

His poems have been published in over 20 literary magazines worldwide, including:

Hudson Review, USA, Skyline, USA, Skald, Wales, La rue Bella, England, The Bards, England, War is a dangerous place, England, The Black Mountain Review, Ireland, ARS Poetica India, India, Metvere Muse, India, Poets International, India, Braquemard, England, Fvirefly Magazine, USA, Pphoo, India, Taj Mahal Review, India, Remark Magazine, USA, Journal Of Anglo-Scandianvian Poetry, England.

His poems appear in the following anthologies:

Shaken & Stirred (Bewrite Books, UK, 2003), Routes – Twelve Poets (Bewrite Books, UK, 2004), A Road Less Traveled (Bewrite Books, UK, 2005), Poetry from the Far Corners (Bewrite Books, UK, 2005), Listening to the birth of crystal (Paulapublishing, 2004) England, Peoplespoet 2 (Paulapublishing, 2005) England, The Review of contemporary poetry (Bluechrome, 2005) England, The book of hopes and dreams (Bluechrome, 2006) England.

Collections "Letters from Portugal" (bewrite books) Bristol, "La Strada" (Lapwing publishers) Belfast, "End of Voyage" (WFP. New York), "Marilyn Monroe remembered" Erbacce Press. Liverpool, "The Fairground" Ranchi India (out of print now).

Contents

The traveller's regrets

He has been a sailor all his life, a traveller trying to find
the boy he left behind, the haste to become an adult
an Autumnal leaf falls into the stream follow its course
but sometimes, there is a tiny inlet where it gets stuck
with other debris before getting loose again and drifting
to where the stream meets a river that ends in the sea
where mighty rivers add nothing but mudbanks that
are full of nutrients and attract edible snappers.
Often, he senses the world ache of the futility of life
to stop for a little while for inaudible contemplation
not to hunger for what he cannot acquire, the ease
of a life well lived.
He thinks the boy will know, who has lived long enough
not to chase rainbows, a fleur-de-lys is but pretty and
disappears from view in a dreamy haze.
Perhaps it was the voyage that mattered and not how
it ends.

a new house

 I saw a photo from a long time, so long it doesn't matter when
the photo was taken; by a couple still youngish with four children
of school age outside a newly constructed house
The year was 1909. looked straight at the camera as was
the norm back then, they had the Sunday's best on
The family was not prosperous but exuded repose of moving
into their own home.
The father looked like having a secure job, perhaps in a bank
or working for a railway company, the new-middle class
that with limited education, could do well and move forward
with enough money to give the children a good start in life.
They didn't know of the many hurdles they would overcome
a war was on the horizon, perhaps the oldest boy would join
and overcome by trench warfare and die of typhus.
We don't know what the future holds but on this day. 1909. was
their happiest day, remembered as long as they lived.

To see forever

I left the ship at the industrial part of the island
 my tour of duty was over and took a taxi to the other side
to take a ferry to town.
At the café near the ferry landing, I drank a few beers glad
my work was done thought about what to do in the coming
 days of freedom from the confinement of life at sea.
Since I had hours to wait, I bought a fishing line, hook and
a sinker, as bait, I used banana skin (it was all I had)
The water was so glass clear it appeared limitless I could
see the fishes swimming about and the seagrass slowly
waved with the mild current.
Bending forward, so fascinating looking down into a watery
world, with water so pure, it was as if the fish was swimming
in the clouds, the thought of the Mâori fable when the sky and
water was one, and life had yet to be born.
Somehow in my dreaming trance, I fell into the sea, people
came running, falsely commiserating over my mishap.
In the backroom of the café, I changed into dry clothes.

A sunny day

The sun shines over the bay
a pilot boat is going out
to take a small coast ship
into Lisbon.
Last night the couple upstairs
was making robust love
plaster fell on our bed like snow
That was ok
love is better than war.
I know the woman
often see her in the lift
she looks chaste and unsmiling
Not that I would tell
about her nightly desire
but the falling plaster
is a worry.

Keeping rabbits

After the German army surrendered, life was tough
the army had employed many to do road work and
repairing bridges, the allies had bombed.
With freedom of movement to roam in the night
followed the theft of food items like the man who
stormed into a bakery waving a rusty Mauser gun
stealing bread; the coal depot needed security
guards as did the sausage producer.
The police force was reduced, and many officers had been
fired since they had been Nazi sympathizers during
the war of occupation; mind, many trickled back
in uniform when trespasses were overlooked.
Of serious crimes, there was one who assaulted women
going home late, knocking them down and stealing
underwear, which back then was a bombastic affair
yet an intimate garment; the newspaper reporting
the case wrote, ladies' items had been stolen
In our time of need, my mother's brother, gave her
two white rabbits, the rabbits soon became many
sweet bunnies, and before we knew the flat was full.
A lady, from the posh part of town, bought the rabbits
her action had not been charitable, she was later
seen wearing a white fur coat.

A girl in Cherbourg

We sat in a bar in Cherbourg a town still struggling after a war
to become just another French coastal town
Sitting with mates from the ship can be tedious, and if you
happen to be a cook, someone is bound to voice a complaint
I went for a walk, in the streets, with few lamps if one adds rain
it was a road suffering after a long war.
In the murk, a place of light, a small café/shop, a few tables
looked inviting in its simplicity; I had coffee and calvados.
A filly came prancing in, tall with long legs, full of youth
Sat down at my table; I asked if she was hungry, and she was
and ate a big plate of stew.
As things are in life, we share a bed for the night.
While she was busy preparing the bed, I sat in a chair thinking
about a short story by Hemingway
about a boxer who owned money to the mafia, and they
were out to kill him, he was tired of running.
I tried to alter the sad ending, but must have fallen asleep, when
waking it was five in the morning, I had to get back
to the ship, my day started at six.
I had a coffee and a calvados to sustain me she the filly
ate a baguette; saw her dance down the street, followed
by the morning breeze promising her a life of happiness.

The ship of dreams

I have never been to Sylhet, Bangladesh it doesn't matter
it was in May, the rain was relentless, and the last Bengal tigers
had drowned in a flood plain and a famous man had been
buried in a led coffin in the Bay of Bengal.
I had been stuck for a week on an elderly bulk ship while
waiting for scrap iron to fill the hulls, the sad rests of once
proud ship the oceans to be cut to pieces with disregard
of the inanimate that had histories untold.
The grisly irony for the elderly ship, it was her last voyage
she had to return to the same noisy, shitty little town
to become scrap iron and nobody gave this great indignity
not a second thought, humanity gave a fuck
On the voyage to Australia, she sank deeper into the sea
then usual otherwise, she ploughed at on at a reduced speed
she was sinking slowly like an aged man in the shallow
end in a swimming pool.
When the sea washed over her decks, authorities were called
and the crew manned the lifeboats, but she didn't go down
right away, she lingered under the sea's surface for days
when the navy came to rescue the crew, she had sunk more.
Having absorbed, over the years, the wishes and hopes of many
She became animate and could sense her surroundings and sense
hurts, the heartache of a crew member whose wife left him
The navy simply torpedoed the ship as a danger to shipping.

The importance of the small things

Out of a crack at the foot of a wall, a tiny baby mouse
blinded by the brightness of this autumnal day
I picked up the new life and put it in the palm of my hand
sensing the warmth, the baby curled up and slept.
To think this tiny animal had a heart, lungs, liver and
so, just like me; living in a world too immense to
grasp other than an outline of space and time.
In less than a week, the baby mouse will be an adult
and since mice do not go for higher education, one
can assume it will not take an interest in the Binary
or no Binary aspect of the struggle to survive.
I put the infant back where it came out of the wall
and upset an Australian, the seller of the house who
hated vermin with a passion.
He claimed mice who came by boat to Australia with
prisoners from the British islands had no enemies
there and was free to breed, they did with a vengeance.
Once he had a farm in Victoria, he didn't give detail
about the location of the farm, only that an army of mice
and eaten his Vietnam pigs and many of his cats.
He sat fire to the dry grass outside the barn, trying to stop
the onslaught, but the fire also set his barn ablaze
his house took fire also, lost everything he did.
The insurers wouldn't pay him compensation because
of his stupidity; angrily, he condemned his countrymen
as vulgar beings.
The man from Australia took up trucking; for two
years crossed the mainland of Oceania killing mice if they
crossed the road.

Having saved up money and also won some monies
at the local lottery, he landed in Lisbon and spoke to a land agent
and bought a farm in Alentejo and specialized in
mule breading, that thrived when he was informed that
breeding mules entails horses and donkeys too.

Where did she go

I knew of her, had seen her in adverts wearing short hair
being, sort of dubious sex, let them guess and smoking
a cigarette with the fragrance of the oriental express, yet
here she sat in a pavement café drinking Pernod, and as
Russian tanks rumbled through the stone cobble streets
she coolly beckoned to me to sit on the chair at her left.
I had a cold beer and lit an American cigarette, feeling tired
had carried a heavy suitcase across the town for a woman
claiming to be an actress, I had hoped she was a spy and
I needed information about troop movements and all
I got was stalk about her upcoming film "La Strada."
On the opposite wall across the café, a movie began
a film about Rome and of a gang of youth stealing bikes
 Vittorio Gassmann had a leading role that was delivered
with aplomb about the question of the value of morality
in a society that has lost its bearing and is crippled by war.
A sudden blackout it might be caused by the Russians
but the restaurant used to this stoppage, producing candles
and the flickering flame from hundreds of candles made
the night romantic; the Monte Carlo woman had vanished
like cigarette ads on the TV screen.

From a photo, 1944

There was a war on the menfolk had gone soldiering
a boy of thirteen and a half was ploughing the field
handling two grey geldings.
The soil looked rich and loose, perfect for Idaho spuds
the big delicious plant ideal for backing.
The boy wore overalls and was absorbed in his work
keeping the plough in a straight line and the horses
the right speed.
Further down the dale, the women near the barn were
hanging up washing, his brother was playing with his dog.
At a further distance, he could see the small town he had
been there, when he was little with his father buying
Ice- cream and drinking soda, guess he was too old now
for this frivolity.
At the end of the field, he stopped to let the horses rest
he drank a bottle of cola and ate a sandwich feeling like
a proper grown-up, a man with great dignity.
He sat thinking of his father and uncle, who had gone to
War in a foreign field, Franch, he thought they had said
And joked about girls, wine and songs to the women's
dislike; he too would join the army if the war lasted
but his mother said he was the only one to plough the field
he had to stay put for now.

The Hegemony

You are not supposed to say "American" anymore it is
a racist like saying "Chinaman" A citizen of the USA doesn't have
to live in the US, but it helps if he lives in Israel
The USA, are master of Europe, let's say the western world
their rule is democracy translated to we dictate, you obey.
With great fanfare, a servant of the outer region of the empire
was summoned to appear before the chief.
The man from the region was hailed as a warrior in the senate
applauded him, and his face covered the front cover
Of The Time Magazine, like Saddam Hussain before him.
It was America with its magnificent display of earnest fakery
promised him to deliver whatever he needed as long as
his needs were America's needs.
But the world knows from experience promises mean little
if there is a policy change, then the friend is a foe overnight
as the world's newspapers sing from the same hymn sheet.

Privately the chief of the western world is worried the enemy
is not leaving the war is costing too much, he must tell
the hero from the beleaguered province to sue for peace.
When the diminutive man is back in Kyiv, he better do as told
or he will, like the man from Libya, end up dead.

Snow is white

He was born in a rather narrow-minded town that had
strict rules for acceptable behaviour, no bars, no restaurant
serving alcohol and no public display of affection.
A Muslim scholar who came to this town by navigational
error, left in a hush, claiming the city was too Pakistani
Houses were painted white, or very light yellow no other
colours were allowed, a rebel, a communist painted his
house red, the law came down hard on him, said his house
was a fire hazard,
had to paint white over the red that made his dwelling look
like a diabetic ulcer.
When new people bought the house, they scrapped off
the old colour painted the house brilliantly white, only to
 discover "white" was no longer a favourite colour.
Any colour would do but white.
Books and articles were written about how terrible the whites
500 years ago, were, colonizing nonwhite countries behaving
cruelly statues of that time were thrown into the sea and great noise
from the righteous people of the day.
The whites took to hating themselves in winter use self-tanning
cream and in summers sat so long time on the beach they got
wrinkled skin and cancers.
But not despair everything is in transition, like men who feel
like women cut off their penises and wear frocks only to discover
nothing had been wrong with them, just being gay.
Too late for them, you might say, but it is also too late for us as
we gladly walk down the path in an oblivious haze towards
the bleaching of the bones.

the long day and Hitler

It is Christmas Eve the TV has nothing to offer but sentimental
crap, where the rich rescue a Christmas for the poor and everyone
in the park and sing while bells chime; no one has bored anyone
by pointing out that it is Jesus's birthday today.

Flicking through the computer's many sites, I came across Hitler's
drawing of Father Christmas, a haunted face casting a side
glance not sure, if someone is making fun of him, the eyes also
tell us of doubt over his profession as a clown.

Hitler didn't travel much, once he stayed in Liverpool for two
years worked as a waiter serving bangers and mash to the local
population the famous sense of humour from that place didn't rub
off on him.

He left, and there was a rumour of him and a pregnant scullery maid.
The next time he journeyed abroad, he went to Paris to see the usual
tourist sites, he didn't enjoy Paris much took the first train home back
to his mountain retreat, where he played with his dog, went for
long walks
and lived in peace until the bombing began.

News is everywhere

I read about a new type of grass growing in Svalbard
making the reindeer happy and fat, not that this is big news
for the polar bear that struggles to learn to live without
ice, to hunt dogs and cats, lose the shiny white fur for
a grimy pelt, smelling of garbage cans.

The howling wolves of the mystic are no more since a way have
been found making (lobotomizing) them into friendly but
silly cubs who want to play with the caribou, who by lapse
has not been told; the good is vet surgeons specializing
in brains are urgently needed.

The good news is the woke brigade will move offensive
paintings of ugly white people smoking cigars, representing
"The man" was replaced with nice Disney pictures of pretty
animals with cute innocent eyes while somewhere out there
the Tasmanian tiger howls in the long night.

The Sea Gull

The one-legged seagull king that lived on the last reef
before the ocean began had lived long, longer than gulls normally do
He came from a sturdy breed that for generations had lived
at the edge of land and sea; they knew things other birds didn't know
On the ferry bound for England the king came on board, I fed it
fine knowing well the king would be back when the ferry re-
turned
Other younger birds wanting the space on the last reef, attacked
the king who never more returned; to the ferry boat they circled
and shrieked in triumph demanding preferential treatment, I gave
them potato peel and saved the best leftovers for the gulls on the
coast of Newcastle
After years of a zero-sum life having no time for anything, I
retired and bought a cabin far inland, but near a lake that had a
wooden pier and a rowing boat, a place where the trout waked
undisturbed.
On the top of the chimney, he sat, the old king, waiting just for me.

Les Miserable

I walked and walked down a steep ravine and came across
a village has forgotten by time by a road that evaded dwellings
A track not trodden among boulders and roofs made of canes.
skinny women with empty breasts sat on the bough of trees
waiting for someone to enter their loss of love
While telling their idiot children in the wet grass to shut up
Oh, crying stones free us from the untidy domestic wilderness
where dogs are too indifferent to muster barks.
Under flat stones, the men are hiding the emptiness of the
existence too much to bear now that the vines take no berry
On this day that has no time, but the endlessness of the gone
Cabbage patch, yellow chickens looking for worms before
the children do because they are hungry too.

The failed suicide.

He sat on the edge of a cliff, feet dangling in the air
the view was spectacular could see as far as only eagles could
could, and to think he had come here to end his life
Sat there, his troubles seemed small alright his wife had
left him, he had to leave their flat, had also lost his job too
and the visiting right to his snotty little children which
suspected was not his in the first place
For work, he could always get another job than the one he had
was a boring, 9 to 5 shifting paper, writing Ok, putting them
on an out-tray.
Now he had a fear of falling laid on his back trying to crawl
upwards, but with his feet over the cliff, he could not get hold
kept slipping down and falling
He didn't fall far, landed in a tree sticking out of a crack and
had grown there for this reason only; clambering to the tree
hang there till rescuers, whose job it is to save people from
themselves came.
Down on the ground and embarrassed, he said, I was not
trying to commit suicide, admired the view, slipped and fell.
Sure, the rescuers said, we have many people, falling from
this cliff when admiring the view.

The end of the year.

The pope is dead, no, not him, but the old one
who liked wearing red hats
There he was, driving his VW around the alps
advancing slowly through the clerical ranks
and suddenly, he was a pope.
Many things happen at the end of this year
a famous Haute Culture woman died a dame
Surely, she must have been surprised so much
fame unasked for.
Don't mention the war!
A low-ranking officer in a secret service end
up a leader of a big country, powerful
like a dictator going to war against windmills.
Not his plan when as a spy walking the night
in Amsterdam.
A very aged man becomes the president
of the USA, going through the political ranks
showing us that mediocrity always pays
and lies win in the end.
Tonight, millions of people will fill the streets
watching fireworks light up the night sky
Anodyne, you say, I'm not so sure if in doubt
ask the people of Ukraine
So, hold tight let the new year commence
wishing a happy birthday to the unborn year.

The day after

This evening saddens me, right now Thailand
celebrates the New Year with fireworks
pathetic lives for a moment lit up by artificial stars
In three hours, time, it is our turn to shine
be blinded by the jollity, of bright objects in the sky
talking about the passing of time.
Time is not going anywhere it is still; we are ants
inside giant cheese holder made of glass, giving life
from an obscure beginning, with one destination
that ends under turf or ashes on a log.
We labour under the illusion life is meaningful and
busy ourselves with trivia that is happenchance.

The day after

This evening saddens me, right now Thailand
celebrates the New Year with fireworks
pathetic lives for a moment lit up by artificial stars
In three hours, time, it is our turn to shine
be blinded by the jollity, of bright objects in the sky
talking about the passing of time.
Time is not going anywhere it is still; we are ants
inside giant cheese holder made of glass, giving life
from an obscure beginning, with one destination
that ends under turf or ashes on a log.
We labour under the illusion life is meaningful and
busy ourselves with trivia that is happenchance.

The days of our discontent

The rain had fallen sharply and heavy flooding roads
fields had become lakes, and cars looked like toys thrown
away by an unrestrained boy child.

From the inside looking out, the sea is calm and subdued
by the cold that makes the sun as ineffective as yesterday's
horseshoe on a smithy's floor.

The forecast is more rain, just as well, the water reservoirs
are after a long rainless period, almost empty, should
tells us o that future wars will be about water, not oi

The wind that blew brought Sahara's sits on the window sill
yet it is better to swallow gritty sand than smell cordite
from an unjust war that thaws the ice on the ground.

Our hearts ran over in sympathy for those who fled the war
we opened our homes and wallets and nailed their banner
on our masts and proudly displayed our love.

As the ghost of inflation sat in, our goodwill struggled rigidly
wallets are empty as a market trader's leather pouch
their banner no longer hangs on flag posts; we are tired.

the old couple

The evening is dark, and the street light tells
the leaves have fallen, except for two stalwarts holding on
 but they will not be there at first light.
On our walk, we stop at a dress shop she admires
a colourful dress as an African, she likes lively attire
 asks me if she still fits this dress; mull over this a bit and say
it will fit you snuggly.
She laughs fondly and tells me; I know nought about women's clothes.
We have grown old together and dislike being apart
 it worries me when she goes into the kitchen to make our
evening meal
We are both aware of the sand, in time glass is nearly empty
 for now, we are lovers in the strand of Nirvana's echo.

Eternal hope

In the ditches of a sandy lane where I once lived
tiny etherical bushes sprung up overnight

Brilliantly green as floating in the air, they were
born by the wind and were a child's first dream.

As dreams, they didn't last long, a week at most
one night they flew away, a fairytale untold.

At dawn, before other animals awoke, rabbits
sat hearing a whisper of time aeons went.

In burrows or in homes, the dream appears
often in the form of a lullaby, we call it hope.

The quest for eternity (Jeff Bezos)

He awoke under the bed; it had been his birthday
and had drunk champagne and eaten Danish pastry
He stretched, feeling stiff, walked to the kitchen, opened
the fridge took out cheese, tomatoes, butter and
A bottle of beer, which thirstily drank.
The cleaning lady had been everything was in order
but wondered where guests had gone and when they left
The house was quiet, not a sound from the street
looking out, he saw cars stopped, some with open doors
like they had been abandoned in haste, must be something
important going on, he thought, walked into the bathroom
had a shower and shaved.
In a bakery/café, he had a sandwich and coffee, which he had
to make himself since no one was around
It dawned on him people had left for a reason unknown
and everything, cars, cigarettes and beer, was free and only
For him to enjoy.
A Rolls Royce that had belonged to the mayor stood in the street
as he had never driven an expensive car before he started
The car, what smooth ride, he thought, but where are the people?
At the plaza, he saw a dog that looked like the one he had
many years ago, called the cur's name, but it growled at him
and ran away, frightened of him.
At an expensive restaurant walked into the kitchen, made
a good meal, and drank fine wine without worrying about paying.
The dog came in, to all friendly now understanding it had
to stick with this person to be fed.
Months went by, he had everything, but he had nothing there
no change, days were the same, he lost interest

in himself stopped shaving and bathing and wore the same pants
and shirt every day as time was endless no point doing anything
Life had lost its meaning; he had to take the matter into his own hands
took the lift up to the top of the building and jumped, but he
descended slowly and softly landed, he broke down and sobbed
He was doomed to live forever as a punishment for his wishes to
Be a master of life and death.

Back under the bed, he went to sleep an eternity away, but the dog
stood outside the bedroom crying, who is to feed it now?

A brief memory

He sat alone under a wooden bridge over a small stream
that (for him) looked deep; usually, a little girl sat the too
but he had banned her and the straw doll she carried
She treated him like a child holding his hand when they
crossed the road.
She had refused to marry him, asking where his dad was
he told her his father lived far away in aficanmission
land, she also asked him what his father was doing
thinking about it, he said, a driver, thinking of the German
a soldier who lived on the farm.
Her mother had said there was no aficanmission land
he was caught telling lies; that girl thought she was
better than him because she was six years old while he
was only four.

Soledar and a salt mine

The mine is enormous and can hide an army of Ukrainian soldiers
the thousands we thought had been killed on the battlefield
The winter is arriving late in this cursed land, no snow falls

The soil doesn't freeze its soft embrace swallows tiger tanks.
From the salt mines, the ghost army arises in the quiet clamour
to vanquish the enemy, elated is the triumph of the deluded.

Flaring fire across the grassland, harvested grain burns bright
but ghosts are forever bloodless; the world is aghast, to see
their triumph thwarted; the magic of victory was but a dream.

A New Day

I have seen flies shake their wings on top of a cistern's lid
I have broken gossamer looking like an angelic mist
and millions of costly pearls glittering in the field
I have seen delicate green bushes spun by clouds
greeting the dawn, when my dog overawed by this
beauty was silent.

Life has many changes and surprises I look out of
the window in a high-rise flat, I see early morning
cars float on diesel-shining asphalt, killing rainbows
The sun, still beyond the horizon, but lit up the sky
where clouds open up like theatrical curtains, shows
 I, the blue heaven as a new day begins.

faraway place

I lived in the interior of the Algarve for many years
in a converted stable made into a cottage that
was smelling of mules when it rained.
After the heat of summers, winters were, if not
Welcome, but accepted as good for the land
Rain and damp, how great to have a wood burner
and a gas stove for cooking when electricity
broke down as it often did.
International problems of the time had a feel
of distance, nothing to with us away from the
the braying crowd and the insanity of pop- culture
Walking in the woods reclaimed by nature
once small homesteads were here, people lived
in need, till they gave up this unequal struggle
and left to find their luck in the USA or Canada
Domestic trees grew wild was oddly shaped
cottages reduced to heaps of stones under
which rabbits had found homes; and to not forget
the boar is not hunted, getting bothersome.
When my dog crossed the railway line and not
looking, I sank into the gloom, the romance had gone
I had not succeeded in my endeavour, time
to leave; eventually, everything comes to an
end, only time remains and is silent.

Summer heat in a town

I was walking in a town on a summer's day
big buildings with underground parking
small houses like Siamese twins.

Soft asphalt, a tree in a miniature garden
had a leafless plant space too small for
a graveyard, the soil was parched.

Once upon a time, the town had a park
it had many trees and a lake for ducks
with threats and bribery, it was sold

Neat houses in a row with just enough
a space between them to park a car
nowhere, the cooling shade under a tree

A grave in Istanbul

He fell down the cargo hold, a long fall
the hold's floor was made of wood and lessened
the brutal slam when he hit bottom.
He got up, waved to us and climbed the iron-
the ladder onto the deck, he said he was ok
He was not ok!
He had about him something vanishing like
his turn of service was over, all he had to do
was packing his suitcase and leaving but lingered
the ship had been his home for many months
He stood on deck on the vanishing day, looking
towards the city's lights, he appeared brittle.
No, he was not hungry smoked cigarettes and
had dreamy eyes.
He was there, but he wasn't there, which made us uneasy
the bright light over his head, a saintly halo.
He went to bed early had been a trying day
In the morning, he was beyond awakening
 a broken body, resting for all eternity.

Recollection of a farm

I hired a car to drive to the farmland
where I spent happy years in my childhood
I stopped by a farmstead looking familiar
A dog came running out and greeted, what is this
am I Jason coming home?
The farm couple came out, they were artists
told me a little boy from the town
it was said he was good with animals
In the kitchen, painted blue, the wife gave me
a slice of bread with blueberry jam
then asked me if I was the little boy.
I told them my story, and they listened well.
A bus was driving past when the dust settled
the farmstead and the couple had disappeared
into the mist of time.

My mother, the communist

My mother was brought up in an orphanage because her father
a confectioner became an alcoholic and lost his job, ended
up looking for work when ships came in and needed dockers
to unload the cargo.
My mother, although working class, was well-read but also
a bit eccentric, she had come to the erroneous conclusion
that only communism (equality in her mind) could bring peace.
It was in one of the papers she read I learned about
Roosevelt's knowledge of the Japanese Pearl Harbor attack.
I was about twelve years old when she dragged me to
a meeting where two Russian "workers" would attend.
They painted a wonderful picture of life in Russia and
showed still films of happy workers at tractor plants extolling
the wonder of the communist regime.
They also showed us the homes of the workers and later
how happy the land workers were breaking out into dance
in their national dress.
I was very young at the time but was not sold on this display
of happiness, mother said I had no imagination.
My mother continued to believe in communism until
the Soviet Union invaded Hungary in 1956.

A dead man and newspapers

It was an extremely cold winter in 1947 the country was ex-
hausted and the German army who did construction work,
building new roads repairing the old ones had kept many civilians
in employment
But the army had surrendered and taken the train home
Mother was not one sitting still; she secured two newspaper
rounds one in the morning and one in the afternoon
I was her helper, more I think, so she could keep an eye on me
In a courtyard, I saw a man sitting on the steps by the entrance
of a house, he sat very still and had ice on his eyebrows and lips
I called my mother, and she said the man had frozen to death, left to
find a shop with a phone (not many people had phones back
then) to ring the police.
The law rang the doorbell a woman opened up; the law said:
"Do you know this man?" She looks at the body and screams
She explains, "he came home drunk; I wouldn't let him in until
he sobered up." Well, one officer said he was sober now they
carried the frozen man, still in a sitting position, into the van.
As I didn't hear the conversation, I made it up.
Why didn't they put the man by the fireside so. he could thaw
and come back to life? No mother said his heart froze;
 the soul had left his body; what is the soul do? I have one.
Yes, you have, like when you tell me lies but insist it is true
when you go to bed, a voice tells you a lied, you can ignore
this voice, but if you do, the inner voice will harden and you
will end up like the drunken man and freeze to death
We're not a religious household, but mother believed Jesus

was the first socialist who took on the Jews and was put to death
What do I know? She also said Santa Claus was an errand boy
for capitalism making us poorer by buying things not needed.

A cabin in the woods

In the flatland near the north-westerly coast where the wind blows hard and is often rainy and cold; my great-grandparents planted many trees that eventually became a forest, not a big forest, but enough to give ease against the wind that sometimes blew roofs off barns and houses.

The perennials took root, although those near the sea were warped Inside the woods, wild animals thrived, foxes, rabbits and many birds

A cabin was built to observe flora and fauna, and it was to a cabin like this, my brother moved in an attempt to hide from the busy world he was suffering from anthropophobia that had got worse as he aged.

He shopped at a grocery shop of the type that stocks many things knew of him when he came, after closing time once a week to buy food the shop also cashed his invalid pension.

The shopkeeper rang me, he had not been seen for weeks the worry was he might be ill and needed help; I went to visit him.

His dog didn't bark when I came and looked starved opened a tin of food meant for my brother, fed the dog as it sat by the door in a futile attempt to guard the entrance.

I knocked on his door and looked to see if the window curtain stirred it didn't; I broke the door down and found him hanged by the smell he had hung there for some time. I called the police to check if he had been a victim of a violent crime; no, it was just another suicide.

Feeling sorry his sad life had ended, death had set him free the only thing

What I could do for him now was to look after his dog.

The candidate

He could have been a contender
for the highest worth
history could be his
but the choice was histrionic

We live in a senile world
the great ones are seen as failures
by the powerful
but history will view the great with gratitude

as the saying goes:
it is better to close down the slaughterhouse
then be a lamb led to slaughter

A despotic country

When Germany lost the war, the civilians
said they didn't know about the atrocity
committed by the Nazis
claimed they didn't know, they knew but
preferred not to know.
When the Israelis meet to this impasse
they cannot blame innocence
as they were willing participants
The slow holocaust of the Palestinians
a land like Israel that reject others' right
and enforces the law of tyranny against
the Palestinians, whose land they took
cannot call itself a democracy.
Israel can only exist by breaking all laws
of human decency, she is Myanmar
of the Middle East.

The Cripple

He lives alone now since his mother died.
A cripple with a built-up shoe drags along like Satan's
cloven foot; his left hand is a claw
He refuses to hide the hand with a glove and wants the world
to see his wounds takes delight when people avert their ....eyes
trying not to see a claw resembling that of a bird.
In his black eyes, flashes of hatred against the living
he reserves his worst venom for those who show empathy
those who offer help.
He travels abroad, to Thailand few times a year for sex
It pleases him to touch the whores, with his claw
See them squirm, and tries to look excited when he fucks them
He is getting older, but the age has not mellowed him
his hatred against women knows no bounds, not since a whore
gave him gonorrhoea, impotently rages against the sound
But most of all, I think he hates himself.

Paradise lost

We danced with thieves with murderous intent
The laughter and fun were screams of utter depravity
Did God assassinate the angels as semen ran
From fruitless loins.
Blood dripped as rain from heaven's elaborate steps
Paradise is lost. Adam molested his sons.
Eleven daughters produced twenty new life a settlement
Began the first in human history
While Eve had a tempestuous affair with the snake of lust.
When Adam got old someone stole his honesty
He had wanted to play the oboe.
From this immoral beginning, animals in the jungle cried
The obscene humans were unstoppable
And now, and now, we wait for the nuclear war to commence

Never look back

For many years he had waited for the bus to take him home
Stark was time, no bus was available, tomorrow perhaps, he could
By a ticket going his way to where his dog waited for him.
So many people who had come and gone, young people fucking
behind the bus shed, he took offence their journey was short
his journey was so much longer
Was it only him who was unlucky for a bus that had to be blue?
Finally, a bus came going his way.
Up a steep hill down into a deep dale, yes, he could see what
he had longed for; at the stop, the dog was a petrified stone
of his house, only the ground wall was left.
He re-entered the bus before its door shut with a blurred shush.
With a sigh, the past was a young man's landscape.

Not like him

No, I'm not a regular good-for-nothing Sisyphus.
Not me, to roll boulders up to the top of a mountain
Only to endlessly fail
I write prose poetry first thing in the morning
Oh, how I write, the dust of spent words resting
On my shoulders
I'm not like Sisyphus, doomed to get up in the morn
I can sleep until eight and often to nine without waking
Up and thinking of some useful themes.
I refuse to be a slave to my obsessions I drink coffee
Hastily eating two toasts, there was something, I have to
Write before reading the news,

The woman from Ukraine

At a nightclub in Montreal, a stripper came on stage pole dancing
I was awkwardly seated and didn't see her well
When her number was over, the public applauded, and she came
to the table and ask why I hadn't looked at her
Before I could stammer an answer, she disappeared.
when leaving, the stripper waited outside, wanting an explanation
Why I had not seen her; over coffee, I told her I had in a mirror on
the opposite wall
at her tiny flat, she undressed, lied in bed and demanded I look at
her pussy, I did and saw a dark forest with a hidden waterfall
only the intrepid would seek to reconnaissance.
Like all beautiful scenery, if looking at it too long, one notices
flaws it gets one-sided the eyes to wander, seeing other things,
perhaps higher up, where mountains ask to be ascended softly.
Satisfied, the stripper slipped under a pink silk sheet and asked
me to remember to switch off the light when leaving

Her birthday.

She awoke before her husband, who was the early riser
she was 80 yrs. old it was her birthday and preparing
a great lunch of filet steak with baked potatoes and salat
A lot of food, her husband said, yes, she lied, I have made
food for several days, and can't cook every day.
She carried the phone in her apron pocket, but it didn't ring.
After a long delay, she decided it was time for luncheon
Lovely food; she had even opened up a bottle of wine.
No, she wasn't hungry; her husband knew why and waited,
she cried.
No one had remembered her birthday; he knew why but
cleared the table, cleaned the dishes and packed the food
away for another day
He couldn't tell her when one gets to be eighty, the living
relatives are so much younger, the distance between the
aged and the younger people is like a vast ocean of years
it is easy to forget.
When he was 84, no one rang, he didn't expect any calls
but for him, being cynical about this matter, he didn't care
 about this, but he felt deeply sorry for his wife.

Red wine and love

A strange woman with a middle-aged faded look.
Fond of red wine and men
She had many who thought she was easy
Tempting her with café dinner
And bottles of wine.
She took what they had to offer she enjoyed
Sex, but not with one
Before they knew snared in her nest
Of lusty love.
Suffering the pain of jealousy hope they would
Be chosen for the day.
The sun is strong, in the Algarve her face
Wrinkled into old age
The men who loved her faded away
She took to drinking cheap wine in dives
Alone she died on a park bench
On one where she so often had made love

The donkey

It was early morning after a night well spent
in someone else's home; a gift of a morning when perfection was
real
On the field in the aroma of spring and splendour, a donkey
grazed, when seeing me hee-hawed and came to the fence
since there are only a few donkeys left in this part of the world
It was used to be petted by people.
After a while, the animal began nibbling pearly green grass
but when I tried to leave, it came back to the fence and brayed
But I could not stay there all day long had a bus to catch
newspapers to buy, and I was out of cigarettes.
Luckily, a farmer on the opposite side of the field opened a gate
et in sheep, the beast lost interest in me and my world.

The contender

I have not met many famous people in my continues life
but I have seen three kings, the first one who, when old
broke his leg for a reason not clear to me and died from
the accident that involved a horse
His son took over, he liked to dress in an admiral uniform
fond of sailing and cocktails, as was Hercules Poirot
when he died, his son became king, a quiet man who has
not done anything legendary.
Of course, they were only famous for being kings in them
little country not like Alan Ladd and Jack Dempsey I saw
a warm summer night in New York; Alan was short and
Jack was tall, and they walked into a bar.
My life is a modest one, hamburger cook when not sitting
In a pub with other pretenders, talking about art, which
we had not seen other than in magazines and books we
had read, thinking we're intellectuals.
Not that I complain, I once took an acting course, but
nothing came out of it, even though friends said I was

talented doing press-ups with one arm behind my back
while drinking a pint of beer.

A vision lost

In a bar, the nightly entertainment is a woman playing
mouth harmonica; she was no "Lou Adler," and
the applause was lukewarm

when she left, her distress hung on her bony shoulders
she walked to the park that has a small lake were
ducks and other loud birds' quacks

the musical lady and I sat on a park bench, talking
about the struggle of getting to the top of our dreams
met by a lacuna of silence.

Suddenly, she threw her harmonica into the lake, for
my next job, I will be a barmaid, no skills needed other
then showing a lot of tits.

I pondered her clear-sightedness and threw my pen
into the lake said, I have tried to write as Hemingway
when my true calling is to be a short-order cook.

Hand in hand, united by our lack of talent, we got up
walked to the unemployment of our futures were
sad dreams appear in the night.

The contented couple

The small window in the cottage had flowery curtains, big
flowers hiding the inside in dunkel harmony
an elegant man with a military bearing sat reading a book about
military history and lost battles, his dog sat chained as it had a
tendency to run away bored because the man in the house didn't
take it for a proper walk in the woods in fear of getting his
trouser legs wet in the tall grass.

The man put his book down, got up, fetched a pen and paper,
calculating how many turnips a battalion man needed for a week.
He had been a captain in the catering corps, moved there since
a scandal when he, on a maneuver, was setting a trap by placing
soldiers on the opposite side of the road; many soldiers had been
wounded
He heard the wife's car; she had been to the hairdresser's she had
a gamey left leg, but the car was an automatic rover car
They lived in a modest cottage since she lost her inheritance, swindled
by a man who said he was a high-ranking officer in the foreign legion
when it turned out he was a waiter who spoke English with a
fake accent.
The captain retired due to nervous exhaustion (incompetence)
but he came from a fine-titled family influential in the upper echelon.
The pair were dim-witted and happily married, but I felt sorry
for the dog that never got a walk in the woods.

Pizzini and Broremann

He used to carry a tiny notebook fitted for his pocket
writing down what he saw on his daily walks in the woods
and also writing rare words in newspapers when sat
in the café by the lake.
Leaves on trees, green grass fledglings trying to fly
many had success others drowned in tiny rainwater pools
life has the habit of crushing us; when we do our best
to be loyal to family and friends.
He once had a sister, generous and kind, who called him
Broremann (little man) because he was a serious child
living in a harsh world not made for kindness, when he
complained, gave him a hug, and told him to shut up.
She had three boys growing up but of poor health
and there was not enough time to pass it on to them
the importance of kindness; motherless they had
to become men in a world that lacked love.
On a page in his notebook, Broremann wrote down
her name put her name next to his heart
reminds him of sisterly love and loyalty that even
mad-men in Sicilia know so well.

Failed humanity

The forest he travelled had many narrow lanes
there was always something new he had not seen before
like the tree that stood out because it was not straight
but bent as a burden had befallen it.
In a clearing where rabbits used to sit to catch
the morning, the sun, a group of strange people had occupied
made a temporary home, resting after a long journey
The leader of the group was an enormous woman dressed
what appeared to be a tent, around her, a smaller strange
looking men looking unfinished
A tall man, presumable the big lady's husband, had three
legs, first I thought he had an enormous penis, noticed
It had a shoe at the end, and his third leg didn't reach
the ground, hence the confusion; they had blind dogs
Distorted with tall back legs like tall rabbits, the dogs
sniffed the air and growled.
The result of a mad scientist who had tried to make a new
Man, and fauna, his failure had been dumped in the woods
I waved at this scrapheap of life, tried to be friendly
but in their eyes, I must have looked hideous, for the dogs
smelling disgusting.

Clearly, I was not welcome and tailed my way out
A week later, I drove the clearing again, the botched humans
had vanished instead, the was a carpet of white butterflies
that disturbed by the sound of my bike, took flight and looked like
a cloud seeking protection from a bigger cumulus mediocre

Home from the sea

The night in the hallway paled into a yellowish screen
showing a black& white home- movie ca. 1963
a memory time machine had sent him back to his years
of youth to meet people long since gone.
A family sat around a dinner table with people he knew.
His 125-year-old father was not there; he never was
a nectar-drinking Colibri, exotic as a Christmas present
never given, the one in a toy shop, a red firetruck with
wooden wheel.
And him? He had gone to the sea, when he returned
it was not the same as before; a certain distance had
emerged after that whenever he came home
from the sea, the distance from them was ever wider.
They had known him as a boy but had not seen him grow.
He sat in the living room, rootless, a stranger they
Somehow were related and spoke politely to him
because they knew he would soon be leaving again.
A nurse shook him gently; are you awake?
Yes, mother, I'm home from the sea.

Pre-surgery

The old man, was up early this morn, drinks a coffee, strong
and has a long hot shower avoiding the black, evil-looking blob
on his chest reminds him of the fragility of life.
Surgery is scheduled at three in the afternoon at a time when
he usually has his afternoon snooze; morning news tells of a strike
at the railways, he has to phone for a taxi early, but secretly
hopes the surgery will be postponed today.
His wife tells him to eat breakfast; he is not hungry but peels
a banana, this insipid versatile fruit that has a bland palate
suitable for a day of surgery and men marching and waving flags
demanding solidarity, better pay and shorter working week.
His wife has ordered food from the café at noon, this madness